The Beautiful Words
Collected Poems

Also by Rena Gerhard

Just Poems
Poetry by Rena Gerhard
The Loving: Selected Poems

The Beautiful Words
Collected Poems

Rena Gerhard

Petronella Press

The Beautiful Words: Collected Poems
Rena Gerhard
© 2025 Fred Gerhard

All rights reserved. No part of this publication may be reproduced, stored in a retrieval system or transmitted in any form or by any means, electronic, mechanical, photocopying, recording or otherwise without prior permission of the publisher:
Petronella Press, 8 Lawrence Street, Ashburnham, MA 01430.

Cover photograph by J. Calvin Gerhard.

ISBN: 979-8-9998858-0-7

CONTENTS

Foreword   xi
Introduction   xv

PART I: JUST POEMS BY ETHELRENE JOHNSON
    Sheeta   3
    King of the Beasts   4
    Conchas   5
    Wild One   6
    The Freedom Men   7
    Madame Tyrant   8
    An Overall View   9
    To a Teacher   10
    The Sabbath - - - and the Movies   11
    The Canoe   13
    Stop to Think   14
    Christmas Firelight Thoughts   15
    Cold Comments   16
    Hate – A Disease   17
    Beauty   18
    Cattle Battle   19
    Weird Winter   20
    Follow!   21
    Lucky   22
    Carpenter, Please Come and Help   23
    He's There   24
    Midnight Forest   25
    The Longhorn   26
    Wolf-Dog   27
    In Loving Memory – Reverend Cox   28
    The Search   29
    The Thriller Killers   30
    A Four-Footed Friend   31
    - To a Woven Hackamore   33

The Bunkhouse Report	34
He Heard Wings	35
Two Fires	37
Strange Steed	38
The Bus	39
"You Don't Know Me, But--"	40
To My Favorite Mother	41
Mystery	42
Perception	43
Earth-Cry	44
Inquiry	45
An Insinuation	46
Earth-Cry (II)	47
Left-Over Dream	48
Kairos	49
Jungle	50
Choice	51
Idyll	52
Coal	53
Campus - 5:15 p.m.	54
Poem to Old Writings	55

PART II: LATER POEMS

Oh Dear	59
Creation	60
Gift Card	61
Lifestream	62
The Perfect Place	63
Accepting Peace	64
Night Walk	65
Mystery	66
Chimera	67
Sudden Fright	68
Reunion	69
The Search	70

On the Subway	71
The Skunk	72
Road Prayer	73
Words	74
Dancers	75
Hush	76
The Star-trimmed Mug; Made in China	77
The Train and Trolley Pile	78
Sorting Screws	79
Childsong	80
Easter House	81
May All Your Swains	82
When the Good Lord Tried to tell us	83
Spring Breaks	84
Absurd	85
The Card	86
Late	87
This Snow	88
Thanksgiving	89
Virtual Mate	90
The Waves	91
Rena's Reading of Sweet "Psalm 16"	92
Traces	95
The Loving	96
The Good Safe Place	97
Supper Will Be Late	98
Sleeping Off the Cold Morning	99
Two Candles Burning	100

PART III: MEMO BOOK POEMS AND PRAYERS

Short Poems	105
The Beautiful Words	108
We Seek Here	109
Plea	110
Laughter	111

The Stream	112
First Mission	113
The Facts	114
Listening	117
Consider Well	116
Visions	117
Prayer	118
To Al Tira	119
Sunday Morn Wake Up Call	120
Epiphany	121
Hearts Yearn	122
Awe	123
Concentration	124
The Natural Response	125
Notes	127
Acknowledgements	131
About the Author	131

Foreword

As a child I remember my mother, Rena Gerhard, reading poems to me like Edward Lear's "The Owl and the Pussy Cat." And later she encouraged me to read poems like Tennyson's "The Charge of the Light Brigade," Coleridge's "The Rime of the Ancient Mariner," and the ancient poem "Beowulf," and many others. She introduced the Bible to me through reading the Psalms of David. Even spiritual life had a door that was poetry. Her love for poetry was infectious and consequently I grew up really loving poems.

She was raised in Pottsville, Pennsylvania, where her father was a shoes salesman, and her mother a clinical psychologist. She recounted, in a small handwritten memoir, that her favorite poems were A. E. Houseman's "When I Was One-and-Twenty," Sir Walter Scott's "Lochinvar," Shelley's "Ozymandias," and Edna St. Vincent Millay's "The Dream" from *Renascence*. Other poets she loved included Rudyard Kipling, Sara Teasdale, Emily Dickinson, Robert Browning, Henry Wadsworth Longfellow, and John Keats.

In this book I have collected all of my mother's poems. She wrote in the 1940s and 1950s, and then again in the 1980s and after. This book is in three sections, Just Poems by Ethelrene Johnson, Later Poems, and Memo Book Poems and Prayers. She gave me permission to publish them in a photocopied hardcover book I sewed and bound by hand. I gave this as a gift to her and my father at Christmas 2005.

She had collected her early poems into a notebook titled *Just Poems by Ethelrene Johnson*. That's the first section. As she says, in her introduction that follows, these are a child's poems, but also include her college poetry. One theme throughout her work is a close relationship with Jesus and faith in God. Some poems here sound young, but occasionally there are startlingly good poems. Check out "Idyll," "Jungle," and the sonnet "Earth-Cry." You will also get a glimpse into her perspective and growth as a young poet in "Poem to Old Writings" where she lets go of language that she felt was old-fashioned:

> *I shall be that of me*
> *Again! I shall be me.*
>
> *No longer old & rut-deep*
> *Riding same and known —*
> *No more!*

The second section is Later Poems. In the 1980s, when I began to get poems published in *Musings*, the poetry column in the local newspaper, *The Reading Eagle*, she began to write again and followed suit. Many of her poems in this section were published from the 1980s through the first decade of the 21st century. There are some amazing poems here like "Oh Dear," "Night Walk," "Sudden Fright," "Reunion," and "Words." During the end of this period she was developing brain cancer, which required an operation and treatment. Following that ordeal she was given a year to live. She went on to live another ten years. Some of her struggles at that time are evident in poems like "Late."

The final section is Memo Book Poems and Prayers. These are her last poems, prayers, and hymn lyrics; she was also a composer. I am moved to see, even in her later years, some stunningly great poems. Look at her facile use of language, economy of words, and emotional impact in poems like "The Beautiful Words," "Plea," and the "Short Poems."

My mother made notes about many of her poems. These are collected at the back of the book and give a glimpse of her life and thoughts about her writings.

I am grateful to my father, J. Calvin Gerhard, for giving me permission to publish my mom's work here. May her poems touch your heart and soul, and encourage you to join the dance presented to you, be it the dance of words, or actual dancing, as she says in "Dancers,"

> *So when will you join the dance?*
> *PLEASE — say you will join the dance!*

Fred C. Gerhard
July 2025

Introduction

Dear Reader,

If you wish to envision your author, I was an only child who loved to read, later, to write.

In the late 1940's – early 1950's I gathered my early poetry. You'll notice several horse-related pieces. At that age I was "horse crazy," influenced by the cowboy culture of the time and especially by the books written by the cowboy Will James who turned to writing after being injured in a rodeo and no longer able to ride.

I see two poems are about teachers.

Some poems speak of loneliness, and one of poets' favorite subjects – unrequited love (Earth Cry).

Not represented here is the hack "commercial" work. In high school girls would come to me in study hall to ask for a poem about them and their current heartthrob, and I'd link their names in a few lines predicting a rosy future for them. Whereupon I'd become ten cents richer and the girls would go off clutching my words, to moon over their crushes. (Fortunately, no copies are extant).

I imagine all poets start by noticing how pleasant rhyme and rhythm are. Then it becomes a game. A poem may spring from a feeling, a theological idea or something as simple as noticing "hey, that rhymes!" *I'll bet* even Shakespeare sat tapping his teeth with his quill while he took the ending of a word and tried each letter of the alphabet in front of it.

Ethel Irene Gerhard
December 2005

The Beautiful Words
Collected Poems

Part I
Just Poems by Ethelrene Johnson
1940s – 1950s

SHEETA

Sleek and smooth is Sheeta,
Her movements like those of water
The black, the beautiful Sheeta
Her grace would shame the otter

Wild and fearless the panther
Sly and wily is she
More cautious than one with the antler
Her wicked eyes slanted to see.

Easily she slinks down the game trail,
Her muscles like liquid steel
Running the hill, pacing the dale
So soft she seems phantom, vapor, unreal

KING OF THE BEASTS

The horizon is touched with rose
The forest is taut with silence
Then through the stillness arose
The baby king's roar of defiance

The creatures lay back and smiled
The forest breathed freely again
The prince would be royally wild
A monarch throughout his domain

Those feathered began with their racket
And Thinkers took up meditation
And hunters came home from their banquet
All honored the princely creation

CONCHAS

Kino! How you gleam and jingle
My saddle was drab and then – bingo!
You sparkle 'gainst the leather black
To catch senoritas you've got a knack.

A plain cream pony like Starweed
Becomes a prancing dashing steed
Through the moon-lit night he dashes
You shimmer in the star-lit splashes.

He'd fight the bit at every bound
Could he not hear your ringing sound
You calm him down whene're he shies
Pulling playfully at your ties.

WILD ONE

The remuda pricks up its ears
The guard looks for the source of its fears
A whinny, haunting and clear
Splits the atmosphere

A mustang, white and free
Sends a whistling plea
The remuda strain at their ropes
To join him sums up their hopes

He's never where any ropes fly
Usually outlined against the sky
A symbol of cunning defiance
The wild one that makes no alliance.

The thunder of hooves in the night
A fearsome sound and sight
With ears laid back the herd rolls by
All fighting hate and frightened eye.

THE FREEDOM MEN

Toughened muscles and callused hands
Proof of the work spent on the lands
Bold-drawn faces with farseeing eyes —
They knew wherein the future lies

Firelight casts its flickering glow
A silent rider on a horse of doe
Moves off into the pitch-black night
To relieve the watch on Pack-Saddle Height

To make the land safe for their kin
Fought the fearless Freedom Men
The voice of youth in our land is heard
Forward's its firm password.

On moves youth in a steady stream
Following after the Freedom Men's dream
Guarding and cherishing Freedom so dear
They fight for the right to which they adhere.

MADAME TYRANT

There she sits upon her throne
Behind her desk — quite safe from stone.

I'd rather go back to my cave
Than to her worded whip be slave.

Quick to attack with onslaught murderous
Under her fire our grades flee from us.

Her questions with slyest craft are spangled.
Her intent — to get us quite entangled.

She might be able to claim success
Were it not that we have one smart genius.

Ah, only to meet her on grounds of my own
For with her to chew I've got a big bone.

AN OVERALL VIEW

We like our drinks with a fizz.
We like our speed with a whizz.
We mark our towels "Hers" and "His."
What a blind racing world this is.

TO A TEACHER

When the drowsy rays of sunlight
Through the schoolroom windows come,
Tinted to a soft orange twilight
By the shades of amber rum.

Then the teacher sighs and stretches,
Hears the echoes of young voices,
A picture, another schoolroom, etches
On the wall, the past rejoices.

On your desk the papers piled
To be corrected and returned,
Marks to be fixed, grades to be filed,
Grades on the sly and grades that were earned.

How empty the room, how silent the air,
The strong horse at the plow has less work and less care.
But who would give up the trusting child's stare
And ask sweet youth's cup to pass on fore'er?

THE SABBATH - - -

A beautiful church-bell, solemn and deep,
Awakens the people from their sleep
The kitchen is lighted and soon breakfast smells
Escape from each kitchen, homes and hotels.

Again the church calls to its people
Who come and fill it up to the steeple
Like sheep they follow their leader's guide
Until they become a wondrous white tide.

Wisely the Shepherd leads his sheep
Though over the bridge they're determined to leap.
Safely back at the end of each day
To His corral He wins them, His way.

A noon-day sun looks down on the feat
And God does too, from His heavenly seat.
The people smile at each other and say,
"Really dear neighbor, it's a wonderful day."

- - - AND THE MOVIES

A beautiful church-bell, solemn and deep
Calls to the people, "Awaken from sleep!"
The people grumble and then roll over
"There goes that church-bell! That proves I'm sober!"

At noon-time the sun looks down with the Lord
To see the preacher, alone and ignored,
He leaves the church and with down-cast eye
Watches the movie-bound throng pass by.

A wisp of conversation reaches God
"The hero fires the church, but that's nothing odd."
A heavenly hand meets a heavenly brow
To wipe 'way the frown that glowers there now

It had happened just as God knew it would
Not a sheep today where a herd once stood
The fear of the Lord, inborn in each
Had been wiped away in one blind-folding speech

THE CANOE

O, light, swift water-skimmer
O winged river prince,
Cutting 'cross the moonlight's shimmer
'Twixt shores of foliage dense.

O Manitou's gift to the Indian man
The white man tries to mimic
The graceful flowing construction plan
That makes you so light and quick.

STOP TO THINK

Where does this running get one?
        this running without a pause,

Nowhere unless you are running
        for a good and a worthy cause.

The world hastens on for a dead-end
        in this highly commercialized age,

A business man running his circuit
        is like a fox in a tread-mill cage.

CHRISTMAS FIRELIGHT THOUGHTS

Our thoughts do often stray afar
At the Christmas season
Our festive spirits often mar
Its real and truest reason.

Christmas is a solemn time
When Christ came down to earth
It is for church and crystal chime
To hail the wondrous birth.

Money-minded mad-men grab
At the Christmas shopper
Purses fat and thin they stab
To line their own purse proper.

So cherish and guard the meaning well
Of this holiday
It doesn't mean a store-wide sale
And packages so gay.

COLD COMMENTS

The weather is freezing,
The fox is a-sneezing.

In my house it's nice and warm
While outside rages one bad storm.

When nature contorts her face,
Then winter takes place.

Te-yippee-yi-ya!
It's turning cold today.

Te-yippee-yi-yo!
Tomorrow it'll snow.

HATE — A DISEASE

Hate burned deep in my heart today,
Seething searing hate.
Hate for school with its beasts of prey,
Scorching fiery hate.

I nearly ruined a summer day
With miserable gnawing hate,
Thinking of how long it was to May
With sickening poisonous hate.

I dreamt at night of the long ordeal
With stubborn fighting hate
Of teachers with mercies of tempered steel
With sullen fiendish hate.

I came on an answer at any rate
With a hopeless wail of hate –
To give in to the written fate
Minus its repulsive writhing hate.

BEAUTY

Tall and stately
Slender yet graceful
Quite sedately
Walk the sorrowful

Color and brightness
Lines and laughter
Join the lightness
For the master

Calm and stillness
Restful sea-scene
Th'elusive movement unceasing
Of a waveling

CATTLE BATTLE

A tense blackness reigns o'er all
And then two orange flashes.
Night again lets her curtain fall
While the echo silence slashes.

Two men breathe a sigh of relief
And then reload and wait
A youth protecting his boss's beef,
An outlaw teasing fate.

Again the guns spit hate and fear,
Again they miss their target.
The outlaw trembles at the cheer
The youth yells — "It's boss Farrget!"

The fatted cattle move pond'rously on
The youth fairly glows with pride
For in his heart there rings a song
And by him rides his bride.

WEIRD WINTER

The cold, white, empty world
With stiff-necked starkness stares
The black trees, grotesquely gnarled,
Point at fear's home lairs.

The wild winds jeer at our attempts
To make friends with the cold.
They scream and mock like eerie imps
They marvel we withhold.

In abstract black and white — the cold
With hostile glittering eyes
Watches and waits to trip the old
With treacherous, crystal ice.

FOLLOW!

Rest and be calm in this troubled time,
Be comforted by the soft hand sublime.
Keep thy impatience in check and tight-reined,
No one can long mock the one God ordained.
Jesus has told us that he is the Way
But ye must do and believe what he has to say.

LUCKY

Off in the distance on a cold wintery night
A shivering colt nickers his thankful delight
As the life-giving fluid his mother supplies
While she turns to shield him from the cold snow that flies.
Two grey wolves pass in a few feet of them
But they catch not the scent of Nature's own gem.
Luck follows "Lucky" for two of his years
When four whistling ropes start his short life of fears.
One gruff cowpoke half-tamed wild Lucky
But during one ride he was bucked clear to 'Tucky.
Now Lucky is monarch of all he surveys
From the wide open plains to the sun's splendid rays
Never aging an hour from the day that he shook
That silly old saddle — he's in legend and book.

CARPENTER, PLEASE COME
AND
HELP

Carpenter, please come and help,
Please lead these weary, stubborn whelps.
Please let us come in child-like faith
Trusting You'll lay down Your lathe.
Please let us trust Thy tender love
And steer us to the home above.
Please come and help, kind Carpenter,
And into humbled hearts do enter.

HE'S THERE

Green and tranquil the forest stands,
Calm forgotten wooded strands.
Rambling paths for troubled minds,
Where the soul communion finds.

Something strong is in the wood,
Something strange, but something good.
Now I know what this thing is,
I walk with Christ, my hand in His.

Twilight creeps on to invade,
Where the sunset's bright rays fade.
Slow am I to leave this church
Made by God of oak and birch.

MIDNIGHT FOREST

Magic is afoot tonight,
The silence seems too tense.
One fears to breathe in case one might
Thus doing, cause offense.

That whispering sigh above your head,
Know you what it means?
A rustling leaf — long brown and dead
Or th' song of Fairy Queens.

The eerie shimmering rigid moon
Hostilely glides aloof.
As if the sun couldn't set too soon,
Plunging from the roof.

The challenging moon is overcome
By the Sovereign Call of the Wild.
That Call will never be heard by some.
They are deaf to its summons mild.

The frigid light of the conquered star
Cascades to the earth.
Where elfin playfellows dance a bar,
Then — Each to an elfin berth!

THE LONGHORN

Swishing tail and rolling eyes
The Longhorn fights the blue-green flies.

With raking horns and slashing hooves
The Longhorn fights the cowpoke's moves.

With jumpy nerves and sudden flights
The Longhorn makes a cowpoke's plights.

With savory smell and juicy meat
The Longhorn meets the need to eat.

WOLF-DOG

The great barren plain spread before him.
Behind him the black timber rose.
At civilization's marked rim
The gray wolf stood out in sharp pose.

Would he cross the wide bleak expanse;
Or become a sled-dog with the rest?
Then off he shot like a war-lance,
He had passed the wilderness' test.

With cold muzzle pointing skyward
He called to his wolfish kin.
Then, hearing an answer, shot forward
To run with the pack once again.

With the pack he hunted and fought
In the forest he made his home.
Through bravery and valor he sought
With a white she-wolf to roam.

Having won her through valor and bravery,
Fair fight having won a fair mate,
He killed only that which was savory
It was only the best that she ate.

For all that I know today
He still guards his home and his lair.
They still roam in the wild North's way
And he still loves his lady fair.

IN LOVING MEMORY — REVEREND COX

God, our help in ages past,
Take him to his rest at last.
He stood the many wounds of hate
'Til, sick, he weakened when 'twas late.

He watched them from their God depart
And then he died of a Broken Heart.
Touch his weeping heart and heal
The bleeding wound that lingers still.

He has done his best to win
Those who fear exposing sin.
All he got for all his pains
Was hate from those who live for gains.

He who was out loving friend
Led us bravely 'til the end.
God, our help in ages past,
Take him to his rest at last.

THE SEARCH

I searched for my best Friend today.
With glad heart I started to look.
The calendar said it was Sunday,
"Worship day," claimed the Good Book.

I entered the wealthy cathedral
And sat on its polished pew.
I waited to find God Eternal
But He'd left there, so I did, too.

I went to the movie that same day,
I eagerly followed the plot.
I hoped I would find Him in that way —
It passed and I missed Him a lot.

Now a small church I entered.
The people were hostile and cold.
All seemed to be quite self-centered
And prejudice had taken hold.

I left the hot city to stroll on
Through country untraveled and wild.
Before the sun was quite gone
Came the Presence so gentle and mild.

I searched for my best Friend today.
With glad heart I started to look.
I couldn't find Him on Broadway.
Instead, in a wooded nook.

THE THRILLER KILLERS

"It's just a movie," they always say,
When they watch the screen.
But couldn't they, for just a day
Forget it's just a scene?

When the action's hard and fast
—The climax on its way
Why must they, in calm contrast
Remind you it's just a play.

Of course we know it's make-believe!
We wouldn't want it real.
We like the thrill that we receive
At this strange "window-sill."

A FOUR-FOOTED FRIEND

The hairs at the nape of my neck arose
Alerted, I quickly turned
With tingling nerves and blood that froze
Two gleaming eyes I discerned.

Too petrified now to flee or to call,
I watched those two embers close in
Then, quite surprised, I gasped as I saw —
A wolf with a moccasin.

He didn't charge and he didn't leap.
He just stood looking at me.
Then he faltered, dropped in a silver-gray heap.
He was starved as I now could see.

He ate and rested for nearly a week
And guarded that deerskin shoe.
Then he pulled at my trousers and slobbered my cheek
And tried to shove out my canoe.

I understood then that he wanted to go,
But he wanted me to go too.
Curiosity got the best of me so
Across the clear lake we flew.

He stood in the prow and pointed the way
Across to the northern shore.
We tugged in the boat and needless to say
I was glad that we'd landed once more.

With joyful barks he bounded ahead.
I shouldered my pack and followed.

We came to a camp where a lad lay abed
In a deep lee the wolf had hollowed.

The lad was a courier with gold in his pouch
And was wounded while guarding the dust.
I took him and laid him upon a soft couch
And sent on that monger of lust.

—TO A WOVEN HACKAMORE

Your sturdy woven strands at last
Have torn and ripped asunder.
And many ghost horse from the past
Have come to mourn their blunder.

Now they weep in their soft way
For having fought so hard.
They all have but one thing to say,
No bits had been their pard.

Your firm and bitless bands have worn
No deep or bloody scar
And yet there're horses still unborn
Who'd fight to keep you far.

The lightest headstall man has made
Has come at last to tear
Into some child's hands to parade
And thence retirement there.

THE BUNKHOUSE REPORT

Was it a horse or was it a deer
Or was it an antelope?
What was the creature that bolted in fear
And traveled at such a high lope?

The moonlight was poor so I couldn't swear
To the creature's actual make,
With my faulty description 'twould only be fair
To warn you — it wasn't a fake,

A dainty-hoofed horse very small and white
— The strangest thing about it —
Don't laugh and guffaw and pick you a fight
But just listen from where you sit.

From its intelligent-looking white brow
A red-tipped ivory horn
Was protruding last night and is doing so now
That horselike head to adorn.

HE HEARD WINGS

The drinking smoking multitude
Were racing on as usual.
They passed one cloaked in solitude
Who's sympathies weren't mutual.

They stopped to jeer the haggard man,
Amazed he would not join them.
Replied he then as Christians can,
He lit the facets of truth's gem.

They hid their sins behind a mask
Until the searching light was out
And then they offered him a flask.
He took and spilled it all about.

Rushed on the rotten crowd again
One 'mongst them sat in poorer thought.
He threw his wine glass at the din.
The stranger's faith had touched and caught.

He jumped the road at Devil's Bridge,
He missed the boulders strewn about.
The Man-with-light called out, "Courage!"
And helped him from the ditch called Doubt.

"Look back now, if you will, and see
From what your soul has been retrieved.
See what your comrade's fate shall be
The leering face — the worst achieved.

No more do turn your face to that,
But watch the glowing light above.

You won't get there and still live fat,
'Tis only won of work and love."

TWO FIRES

A fire is blazing somewhere
'Cause I can see the haze.
It's not a sullen red glare,
But white and pure with praise.

There's a mighty lull in waters
An' a mighty rush of winds,
And all true sons and daughters
Of God lose all their sins.

But they that grinned derision
An' flaunted foul delights
Have made their rash decision
And handed Hell its rights.

Another fire is burning
An' I can see its haze.
I know what they are earning
Though it does not meet my gaze.

STRANGE STEED

When the dusk comes flowing in
Trailing shy stars at her heel,
When the blazoned sun has been,
And when nothing seems quite real,
Listen then.

When the world is done in grays
By the sky-pearl called the Moon,
And the lavish night arrays
Nocturnal wand'rers in her June,
He neighs!

When the wise had gone to bed
To receive their well-earned rest,
Then I watched him as he fed,
And I sat his back, a guest
Instead.

THE BUS

The important roar and snort of a bus,
The impatient way it sighs at the light,
The way it ignores the car-sized fuss,
The flash of its sides in a light at night:

These make me ignore the gasoline smell;
The troubles of the tedious ride.
These hold a certain "Return!" smell
That changes like the sea's own tide.

"YOU DON'T KNOW ME, BUT - -"

Somebody somewhere is looking to you,
Not for clothing or food or brick clay,
But he really is looking you through and through,
For he's building his life on your Way.

TO MY FAVORITE MOTHER

Mamacita, dearest one,
Depth of love and Warmth of fun,
Counterpart and Complement,
May thy Day be heaven-sent.

Madre mía, mother mine,
Happiness be always thine,
Realistic optimism,
Faith, love, hope, and sturdy wisdom.

MYSTERY

Like the prisms of an opal,
Never changing nor the same —
Living paradox in heart-fall —
I hate, I like — yet you remain.

Like a shimm'ring violin-song
Lost to ear but truly kept,
Seeming gone, but never quite gone —
Whom of you shall I accept?

PERCEPTION

There isn't another feeling like
Being one small human
When there's a too-white seashell
There in the Sky
And music in your ears, so very gold
It's almost Red.
It isn't fair — yet, incredibly,
A man is big enough to hold the
Light with those two tiny
Cups called Eyes,
And then there's just enough of him
Left over to catch the music.

EARTH-CRY

Far vacillating star who makes
A shining and a bitter glow,
A shimmering song in vacuum lakes,
A crystal mace, a chill blue flow,
Give audience to a breath of dust
Nor sheathe yourself in centuries.
Why fascinate a mortal just?
Why make it feel such strange unease —
Let fatal glance—too cherished—strike
A stinging love—too deep for it.
Why cherish thus, all human-like,
A glance, O creature sadly smit,
While knowledge burdens every hour
That only planets charm a star?

INQUIRY

"What is love, oh, what is love?" she cried,
"A feeling gentle toward the one you love?
A feeling strong to ward off stings for him?
A feeling safe through all his flick'ring moods?
A feeling free while in his prisoning palm?
Oh tell me, for I do not know of love."

AN INSINUATION

                                              ("Murderer!")
In the cry-scream of a child's despair.
'Turned with helpless wrath and hopeless groan—
Earth to warn — An anthology alone
Bearing Caesar to an empty square.

                                                ("Murderer!")
Trade winds of a friendship Beauty bore
Streaking to an haven walled with fjords,
Safe from Hatred's high-held wooden swords.
Then the sneered suggestion — nothing more.

                                                ("Murderer!")
Static-words struck unexpected pain.
Beauty's twisted smile; Her tears, so rare —
Then 'twould poison Him with death-dark stare
But I stab poor Beauty, hating Cain!

EARTH-CRY (II)

Far vacillating star who has
A shining and a bitter glow,
A shimmering song in vacuum lakes,
A crystal mace, a flow of blue,
Give audience to a breath of dust
Nor sheathe yourself in centuries.
Why fascinate a mortal just?
Why make it feel such strangeness rise —
Let fatal glance — too cherished — strike
A stinging love — too deep for it?
Why cherish thus, in human streak,
A glance, O creature smitten yet
While knowledge burdens every hour
This spell-bound slave stares willessly
That only planets charm a star?
O distant star, who wilelessly
Has trapped the mind of tiny man,
Release him from this senseless grip
That draws him to the airless main
Where everlasting sleeps do drift.

LEFT-OVER DREAM

My couch was fragile floating leaf;
My sleep was mewing winds.
My storm-green nap was cool and sweet —
And wrapped in silky wings.

The musty, matted vines of thought
Were torn by stumbling dreams
That cut the chafing thongs of doubts
And sang in soothing drone.

And there were blade-tongued, rasp-limbed things
With terrible, silent tread,
And always eyes, white blinking ring,
Watched, reasonless, for death.

And then I wished a tree — I leapt
And touched rough, living bark.
I went too high, but then I laughed
In Afric slumber far.

Spring-warm half-timbered Tudor day —
Dear-cherished Ultimate.
I will not wake or let this fade —
Left-over dream centric!

KAIROS

She stands in life without sight of it.
Eyes of her fix with watching.
She looks for Kairos.
She must be ready —
For Kairos.

She moves through life without touch of it.
Hands of her stiffen from stillness.
She waits for Kairos.
She must be ready —
For Kairos.

She strides past life without heed for it.
Ears of her ache for ultrasonics.
She listens for Kairos.
She must be ready —
For Kairos.

She reaches death without living.
Kairos in life has been none of her.
She leaves Chronos.
She must be ready —
Kairos.

JUNGLE

Jungles of danger lie around

She is as a blind person
Set about with quicksand.
— Nowhere safe to turn
— No hand true to grasp
— No voice clear to guide
Through the invisible
        Jungle.

And turning, she frets
tries
        steps
                is sure

                                      falls.

CHOICE

Pray naught else be like regret!
Such unholy grief —
Thoughts which should have died squirm free.
Decision idly lacerates
The mind that struck and tempered it —
The other way — the other chance — the haunting
Why oh why oh why — ever!

Shun hope and suck in scream
Poor blind . . .

                Perhaps a dream will hear . . .

IDYLL

Uninspired inspiration!
    This I have waited.
    This I have fought.
        The ticking of a clock?
        The singing of a lamp?

        The peace of her sleep?
Yes. The peace of her sleep,
    And the sturdy friendship . . .
        the trust — vulnerable —
    And the peace —
        the peace of her sleep.

Quiverless and full, her sleep . . .
    A mist that laps around my
        wakefulness . . .
    An ether without panic.
    Life tolerating death.

I have a trust, a faith . . .
I too, shall sleep
    . . . perhaps, more soundly . . .

COAL

Will no one love the coal-banks now?
Piles of dullness shift (coal) these
Glacial floes of jetsam (coal), newly
Cracked from manless slough (coal).

Red-sweatered second grader thuds
His mighty plaything (coal), does not see
Dirty beauty — long-dead death (coal),
Starving out its thief.

Hope and ache and will chip through
Black strength (coal), under-earth.
Blood, bones, forests (coal), man-unthought,
Save as memorial mountained COAL.

She (that cleans house hates
Griminess (coal); shifting grit)
Shakes thin fist, can't rouse
Post-pain stupor of black heat.

WE CANNOT SHAKE ITS
      GIANT SLUMBER.

CAMPUS — 5:15 P.M.

Ring, Angelus. Do not tell
A skeptic called a chaplain
Sits beneath you

Death
Real death

I am not afraid; I knew the
Suffocation of his Lazarus-gaze —
"Doubt for the sake of doubt"

Praise be to God!
There was a man
From Thailand
Who left with me (back to dorms, Thursday)

His brown face smiled and there was God
He said, "It works.
Christianity works when all
The words are done and I
Walk out to live."

POEM TO OLD WRITINGS

How good to be tired,
Tired
And sit in sun and know
From writings
What I was and felt

Howdo, me.
Why, much forgot is worth
Regathering
I shall be that of me
Again! I shall be me.

No longer old & rut-deep
Riding same and known —
No more!

Thank God there're parts of
me (& thee as well) I do not
always know.
      And now consign my
tired-out self to be forgot
         And dug up after rains.

Part II
Later Poems
1980s – 2000s

OH DEAR

I'm not at all what I used to be —
Has anyone seen where I left me?
The glass reflects the passing shell;
The ruins of Troy lie where they fell.
Leave powdered Helen in a heap?
or shall I sweep?

CREATION

She made herself
out of pale lipstick
gypsy shawl
peasant blouse
added lace
stitching memories
latticing pleasantly;
naïve shoes
worn to fit
remembering country dances

GIFT CARD

They're dancing around in the cage of my mind,
The words and their twins writ for you to find!
Anniversary, birthday, Christmas — all share
The occasional chance to say that I care.

LIFESTREAM

The piping flute
Her dream
His cello counterpoint
Knowing pipes
And plumb —
Rankering tax
Singers swell in chorus
A cricket frenzy
Round on round
With piteous
Ensamples
Dreaded dreadful

Government
We
Swayed as grasses
In riptide

Rooted in old rope
The middle —
Where most people
Live in hope
Cry and love
And
Sift and vote!

THE PERFECT PLACE

I always feel successful when I've just cleaned up my space —
A box or niche for everything and each is in its place.

And yet I know two weeks from now there'll be an anguished howl —
We've got to find that paper's clever newly-hidden file!

ACCEPTING PEACE

'Neath hushed breathing
in the sepia evening,
Lavenders lap along the creeping
      indigo
and seep along gray limbs
of black, black walnuts

Behold the small gray gardener
blended to her branch,
her convex hammock.
Lids droop, oval; almond—
over tired black-liquid orbs,
ever, ever lower . . . finest slits.

The twilit squirrel stares,
faithful witness
to the down-slip of our common Star,
abruptly
knows she's done—
must turn
on slender graceful ankle
and glide, silent,
to her quiet nest.

NIGHT WALK

All day
Maples shatter sun
to ruby, cat's eye yellow; gold.
Prismed vision —
What a way to meet our nearest star!

Living through my night walk
She's sleeping standing up
Having dreamed her children
to the wind —
Now verging on
Relinquishing lavish
Rough brown blankets crackling down
To mold, warm, live with
Microcosmic engines.

Queens in neat rows
Asleep on their feet
Yet nursing their babes
Most naturally.

MYSTERY

Don't you just hate when you clean out a drawer
And not all things fit that fit before!

CHIMERA

                                         — just there
Between river and road —
No, no! To the left of that rock!

An invisible line
A century ago
        — some fought to move
        — more died to save
That line you can't see —

                                          — just there
Between river and road —
No, no! To the left of that rock!

Later scholars will quarrel, ask where,
None living will know
Nor anyone care —
        No, no one will . . . care.

SUDDEN FRIGHT

Too long in one place
Like a tree
I play Russian Roulette
With the spinning world.
My refugee mind
Plans to flee,
Tracks the solitaire Moon
through the fingering clouds
Flying free.

REUNION

Glistening white in merciless sun
A meeting of snails
Count back-streaks, seeking match.
Touched antennae retract . . .
      rehatch.

"Nice to see you again"
      sound catch, song-snatch . . .
Jig-cut memory, frayed to fuzz
    idly stirs cindered loves,
      rattles bones of dried fears—
By dinner, all glad
    of the armoring years.

Scarab-like they roll their fables,
      wistful of others' seemed eternity
All leave wrapped in china smiles
    to drop this newest pearl
      'midst treasures, truths and trials.

THE SEARCH

I went a-searching through my dreams
Down fragrances, along thought streams —
In mists, cold echoes clop-clopped, while soft shoe
Through broken cobwebs rainbowed dew.

ON THE SUBWAY

I saw them on a subway
Fling into seats
Ears plugged with radio,
Eyes slid out of focus.
One line crimped a forehead
(would not leave a trace —
such dewy skin!)
I cannot speak —
("Don't talk to strangers—"
Having mothers, we both know!)
Yet I ache to ask —
"Tomorrow Man,
what do you hear?
That line — a trace
of hate words
Trampolining in your ears?
Or puzzle-tracked
philosophies to stitch
your memories to life with
Threads of human hope?"
Forgivably, humbly, to the dear God above
I pray you hear
Love.

THE SKUNK

It's hard to be cross at a skunk —
She can't help she got scared and stunk.
She sprinkled the breezes
With defensive sneezes
And it's better'n a bitten-out chunk!

ROAD PRAYER

Novice on the highway of
Blurring signs and
Sudden lights
And I am praying
Our Father
Who knew this road
Before it was
Grant me noticing
Ban salient thoughts
Pardon my worried frown
And oh, above all —
Don't let me knock anything down!

WORDS

I thought we were talking side by side
Didn't know you were in front
Taking my words on the chin
      — words never meant to hurt
      — never meant to bruise
      — words meant to walk side by side with yours
And in the evening afterglow,
In the early fireplace light
You quietly crying
And I didn't know . . .

DANCERS

Dinosaurs dance sedately.
Because of their weight and their delicate toes.
Their walnut-sized brains and their clattering clothes,
Dinosaurs dance sedately.

BUT dreamers all dance in their minds.
Because of perhapsing and pop-corny hope,
And inside-out thoughts of incredible scope,
Dreamers all dance in their minds.

When will YOU join the dance?
Oh, that's what the earth's for —
A wild ballroom-dance floor
So when will you join the dance?
PLEASE — say you will join the dance!

HUSH

Hush! Hush!
"Hush-Hush-Hush"
Brushes his teeth with a vegetable brush
Walks all night on a mountain of mush
Tickles small owls till they sing like a thrush —
That's Baby's night-friend,
"Hush-Hush-Hush"!

THE STAR-TRIMMED MUG; MADE IN CHINA

Fingers not quite
      colored white,
Number: five
      built to survive,
Gently shaped
      this smooth blue brink
      from which I drink.

Her heav'n like mine wears stars
She's loved both Moon and Mars
      with eyes like mine,
And we divine
Shared joy:
This toy.

THE TRAIN AND TROLLEY PILE

It is our music!
How it fills our house —
Tread with ginger feet
Our many-mansional paper jungle —
My enemy and my friend the paper moat
       obsequious
       encroaching
       undercrunching
       web words knitting us
       to tons of metal sliding screeching people boxes —
Footprints crackle — this is our home;
                         this is its anthem —
       our litanies' appoggiatura
       of shaved-wood surf — our music.

SORTING SCREWS

Delicious
Absorbing —
Simple work — finding, filling
 patterns
How are you going to do this?
I don't know.
Let me do it awhile
then I will tell you
How.
If you've tasted the trance
It will flash in your glance.

CHILDSONG

They're keeping the sun just over the hill
But no matter how fast we ride
He's gone to bed
(My mother has said)
When we get to the other side.

The drive is long and so is our song,
The verses get mixed in my head —
I plan to say reams
But they turn to dreams
Woven of quicksilver thread.

EASTER HOUSE

Two china rabbits, out again,
  fix soft-eyed stares like wonder
  (day night day night day night day)
  and see no miracle embodied large in th'candle-wax smooth pink
        and very perfect Egg betwixt.

Meanwhile mid-window parade past latches
  drake, duck, duckling, smallest duck
  (predestined to devotion man and maiden may much envy)
  drenched in brilliant dawn.

Yet only hearts in human clay will ever see the hallowing light,
  so different from the mundane ray our little star pours out
        erasing night.

MAY ALL YOUR SWAINS

"May all your swains
As you pass by
Sigh with pity
For th' eddying breeze
Bereft of such a
        Pretty!"

"WHEN THE GOOD LORD TRIED TO TELL US"

When the Good Lord tried to tell us
What God was really like —
When He and the twelve disciples
Were on a country hike —

He looked around this Earth.
"An example! Ah! But who?"
and then He saw a Father —
A good Dad — just like
      YOU!
Happy Father's Day!

SPRING BREAKS

Not in the first race of
        chipmunk strife
Nor in the startled crocii's
        pastels palette rife
Nor thrilling trill of
        lark and wren accord —

But in the Spring
        of my beloved Lord
          out of the ground —
           Heavenbound —

Blazing the Way
        for my rejoicing soul
          to rise above —
        Awash in Love

ABSURD

"Absurd!" —
What a wonderful word!
A laugh that bursts
Like water balloons.
Drenched we are —
We've been buffoons! —
Shoring up crazy-quilt
Government guilt,
        prettily pricking,
        pettily picking . . .
Don't point your finger at me "Kew-Kew"
Or I will see They jail You-You!

THE CARD

It's just posterboard and ink
  and a verse thousands read and think
    "Just right!"
They've bought and sent,
  seeing the people they love
  or through duty would honor
  or some barely known to surprise with print —
  or people they hate!
      but hate more giving cause
      to feel superior and berate
      this most brusque purchaser of my card!

My card — I see you handling it —
Your hands cup it —
It's cupped in your hands
  Like a candle flame you would guard
And you smile over its edge
Touched by the well-wrought words
  of the clever well-paid wordsmith
  and the visions once more well-expressed
      in colored ink —
        landscapes,
        still lifes,
        improbable cats, bears,
            dogs or mice —

But on this bit of posterboard — this fragile craft —
  so easy to misconstrue
  rides a trembling heart
      from me to you.

LATE

Soft I've padded well past midnight.
Now I wade against the unseen current
  of the River Lethe that floods my living room
      flowing invisible around me
      and I've breathed its ethers

Oh, just a paragraph — a small one —
      this letter's nearly done.
I know the words, have spelt them
      since 3rd Grade!
Yet now rebel fingers have drawn "M"
      where I said "W"!
And how did "p" get there,
      trolling below the line in place of the "b"
      I ordered a scant minute ago!

Once more I floss, staring mindless
  at the bright-voiced newscaster
  who's been struggling to gain my attention,
  all peppermint perkiness, as though understanding
  it will be a steep climb — these glass trails
  of my neuron's paths connecting their way down
      to the Miracle of Sleep.

THIS SNOW

This snow I do not think we'll have to move
        but only love —
Heirloom lace spread perfectly smooth,
        the tablecloth land below
        meant to show!

Finest stitch of sparrow hops
        link bush to branch to porch to perch
While down white canyons —
        Last week's blizzard
                Laid aside awaiting thaws —
Squirrel-leap and rabbit dart
        basting stitch the path of paws.

All join in crochet whorls to ring
  the water
  And create star-ray leads
  approaching to the seeds.

THANKSGIVING

Thanksgiving evening, around the cleared table
Brains strain
for the game,
  cards a-blur —
While the lovely lilting
  river of familiar voices
  passes over me and
  I drown, not caring,
  For I'm finding the dream stream
      of voices from other
      feasts floating by,
      smiles left in my mind
          by dear faces long gone,
      A sunset of sweet music left in my ears alone,
      visions of dining rooms
          in houses long since sold, changed, charming yet.
          I roam them so often
      my inner glance caressing, happy.
Meanwhile this fantasy NOW
    is playing along like a TV
someone forgot to turn off.

VIRTUAL MATE
(The Computer Widow's Lament)
(or Computer After-laughter)

I wonder
      (If he dies)
Can I have an outstanding
      understanding
With a taxidermist specialist
      (a standing underwritten
      special outing—via taxi,
      natur'lly)
Actually to convey him thither
      — and back
And sit him up so straight
      — (the Late)
— he is so straight a sitter
Entranced, enhanced, advanced
      finger on mouse,
Eyes glazed, gaze hazed
      but just a little —
So life-like
      (just don't banter —
      he won't answer —)
He'll look so wise
In such disguise

THE WAVES

    NPR on the car radio manifests
        in rising and falling cadences —
            a poem I can barely hear,
                perfectly mirrored in the
                    undulating back of a black cat
                I can barely see.

    His stalking makes a
        counterpoint to the
        universal swaying, April winds
        combing roadside grasses.

RENA'S READING OF SWEET "PSALM 16"

I.

I said to Him:
        You are my Lord; I have no other help but yours.
        I want the company of those who love you —
            they are the true nobility.

Those choosing other gods shall be filled with
        sorrow; I will not offer the sacrifices they
        do, or even speak the names of their gods.

The Lord Himself is my inheritance, my prize,
        my food and drink; my highest joy.

He guards all that is mine . . . I will fall heir to pleasant brooks
        and meadows.

I will bless the Lord Who counsels me; He
        gives me wisdom in the night.
        He tells me what to do.

I am always thinking of Him, and because He is
        so near I never need stumble or fall —
  Heart, body and soul are filled with joy.

Lord,
        You will not leave me among dead men.

                You let me feel the joys of Life, the exquisite
                      pleasure of Your own eternal Presence.

Save me, dear God — I have come to you for refuge.

II.

I said to Him,
        You are my Lord, I have no other help.
        I would mingle with your followers
                here and now.

Those choosing hollow gods shall reap sorrow —
Your good gifts I will not give up to please
Idols whose names shall not even pollute
        my mouth.

You Yourself are my inheritance, my
        high prize, my food, my drink; my
        highest joy
                You have set my boundaries and
                I see it is good.

I would call down blessings upon you,
a Source of Blessings. In prayers
and dreams You bring me wisdom
in the night. I wake up knowing what to do.

TRACES

No stone will ever show
        how lightly dance his feet
Nor reflect how sweet
        his laughter as it bells
                in my ears
        No clever statue catch
            his warming smile!
And though I may try to
write of him, look through the
hollows between the words & reality
        & see as much

THE LOVING

Diamond-flashing, opal-gleamed —
    Mothers' loving shines
    Strong in those years of dust-disturbing
    Sandal prints where sons met foes
    and daughters' hot tears rained on folded clothing
Yet most in peace-bestowing, blessing-counting
    dream-beseeching
    prayers that climb her steepled hands
    while teaching, always teaching
    sons and daughters
    Mothers' mothers' mothers'
    dazzled awe
    at Heaven's Love
    and Love's bright call.

THE GOOD SAFE PLACE

I remember just yesterday I thought
I must put that in a
    Good Safe Place.

Now where was that
    Good Safe Place!

After searching long & hard
    for the good safe place

I've begun to wonder
    what it was I'd thought
        I'd put in such
            a good safe place.
Ah well — at least it's in a good safe place.

Some future
    archaeologist will take a
fine bristled brush and find the little treasure and
    the wondering
        will live on.

SUPPER WILL BE LATE

Stand Still Time!
Parade Rest petulant my demand!

Can't you see
        I've a new book of poems in hand
Insistent entreaties
        luring rhyme drumbeats
                to new opened doors
I've entered thought through your gates
        and my feet are happily
bemired in a Stranger's river
of words

The Lute in my heart
        still reverberates with
                his songs
It's Stand Still Time
. . .
O, supper will be late.

SLEEPING OFF THE COLD MORNING

Sleeping off the cold morning
In a warm woolly blanket and the arms of my love,
Planning in a dreamy way
What we will do in the warm noon-day . . .
      Eden in a fragile night
      Adam in the first sunlight
      Paradise with thee, my love —
      Downy quilt and stars above . . .

Sleeping in and dreaming in the dawn —
Kiss me now before I wake.
Share with me the still day-break
      When the herald birds are hushed . . .

      In the arms of my love —
      In the arms of my love, planning
What we shall do in the warm noon-day.

TWO CANDLES BURNING

Two candles burning, dispelling the night —
Where does one flame end?
Wick, wax, and fire blend
Into one light.

See the light, sweet and warm, where there were two?
Mingling and melting,
Soaring and lilting,
Dancing life through.

Part III
Memo Book Poems and Prayers
Last Poems

SHORT POEMS

work rhythm gets going and you hate
to stop even though you ache . . .
you're "in the swing"

☼

Dismayed by sudden visions
of what was wrong with what
we were doing

☼

Any requests, Lord? Anything
You'd like me to sing?

☼

To the God who thought it would
be a nice touch to grace our days
with laughter

☼

Defuse the ticking bombs
of nurtured hate

☼

My cup is full of memories,
and only some are sweet

☼

with her feelings all
boarded up against
the gray sky day

☼

a song I thought I'd
never remember
goes dancing
through my mind

☼

singing with
mosquito per-
sistence

Sometimes mind goes
round like idle wheel
of bike tied to a car

THE BEAUTIFUL WORDS

Sometimes I stand at the door of a dark night
and whistle,
and the beautiful words come running.
Then times come for the empty search
of well-trod ground
of dank hollow wells
where I cannot find a sound,
oh — except these
tool words
someone left lying
in a broken box.

WE SEEK HERE

We seek here the wild and Living Stream
That bright river that gladdens the City of God!
We desire the clear refreshing Stream
such as Moses unleashed with the lash of his rod —
Somewhere it flows!
Somewhere it flows!
Somewhere it flows!

Faint it chimes through our dark forest — days.
How it sparkles with reason, it dances with hope,
glints between tall stony grating days.
But we thrill to its thunder and gasp at its scope,
Somewhere it flows!
Somewhere it flows!
Somewhere it flows!

Pilgrim, cool your face at this Sweet Spring!
Drench yourself, safely lost in God's will to revive!
Quest to share! This is the Living Spring,
more abundantly blessing as share it we strive.
This Jesus knows!
This Jesus knows!
This Jesus knows!

PLEA

Caught in the act
Between being and becoming
Frozen by the flash of Thy
Lightning . . .
Defenseless as wild animals
alarmed . . .
O, judge most mercifully Lord!

LAUGHTER

"Are you glad to be saved?
Let it show!
Are you glad to be loved?
Let it grow!"
Effervescent happiness
will start to grow inside —
don't keep the lid on —

Let it out in —
Laughter!

THE STREAM

I am looking for the Stream
       the Clear Stream
       the Refreshing Stream
       the Curiously Satisfying Stream
O — somewhere it flows!

Have you heard its voice
 in the forests of your days
       the tall stony days
       the shoulder-to-shoulder days
       the grim, grimy grating days?
O — somewhere it flows!

Have you cooled your face
 at the Stream?
       Its living waters restore reason
       Its living waters revive hope
       Its living waters spawn joy
O Jesus knows where it flows.

FIRST MISSION

Jesus — Your Lord and
mine — isn't inter-
ested in excuses —
Just "go thou and
sin no more" — He's
said it o'er and o'er!

THE FACTS

The facts don't matter
the facts don't count
because my God and I are
determined to change them

Everything is in flux
in seemingly solid metals
electrons twist into line and dance
to the tune of the magnet
and yesterday's headlines
richly deserve to line
today's bird cages!

LISTENING

If God called, could
I hear the ringing over
the TV?
The box that makes my head to
ache was loudly selling pain relief,
O please repeat again what
You just said!

CONSIDER WELL

Were I a saint and mine
enemy prayed for
me to intercede on
his behalf — from
whence would come
my strength to do it?

Pray for your enemies
and those who persecute
you so that you may
be sons of your
Father who is in heaven
        If mine enemy
had fallen among
thieves on these, our roads
to Jericho . . .
for these
are the days that try our souls
and these are
the ways
Would you
want to fall
into the hands of
an enemy no one
had prayed for?

VISIONS

Beyond the cross,
Lord take me
Beyond the cross
Grant me visions of
heaven
Set my sights on
glad visions of
      thy glorious goals
for my life.
      Show me where thy
footsteps disturb the
world now

PRAYER

Dear Lord God, to
whom the ordering of the
Universe at Creation was
no problem, please help us
set the priorities on our
lives — help us draw near
to Thee diving the quiet
pools in our lives, so that
when we are thrust into
sudden rapids we can feel
sure that Thou and we are
in the same boat. We ask it
in the name of Jesus who
slept peacefully in the
storm-rocked boat, but
who was instantly obeyed
when He told the winds
to knock it off! Amen

TO AL TIRA

Let us tune our harps
      and hearts to sing God's
      praise
Thou hast let us work for
      Thy kingdom seven days
      Seven since we met to
      Learn and share
      Seven! Thank you
      for all Thy care!

SUNDAY MORN WAKE UP CALL

I was glad, I was glad
when they said unto me
let us go to the house
of the Lord . . .
I was glad, I was glad
when they said unto me
let us go to the house
of the Lord . . .
        let us go to the house
        of the Lord

EPIPHANY

God speaks. Listen — this has worth
See the wild display —
Fire unfurls to carpet Earth
white tempests round Him play

HEARTS YEARN

Am I singing songs Lord,
when I should be listening?
Thou art always listening
for the heart felt prayer
      And Thy hearing
         lifts our souls — we
         feel Thee care
We call Thee "God"
as though a word could hold Thee
Thou dost befriend
We comprehend, and so our
hearts yearn boldly

AWE

Awesome God!
Awestruck worshippers!
Our nostrils tingling with
Incense of mystery
stabbed through by brilliant truths
Mingle in this thy
Sanctuary

CONCENTRATION

One step at a time,
one step at a time.
Lord keep my mind
on what I'm
doing one step
at a time!

THE NATURAL RESPONSE

This day, this day
in Paradise with Thee
we came to worship Thee
This day, this day
accept our worship free

NOTES

The Early Poems were collected in a book titled *Just Poems* by Ethelrene Johnson in 1955.

All of Rena's poems were first hand-published and hardbound by Fred Gerhard with Rena's permission and proofreading. *Poetry by Rena Gerhard* was published in 2005 and included her introduction.

"Absurd" was written at Electric City Trolley Museum May 12, 2002 (Mother's Day) and published in *Musings* August 11, 2002.

"Accepting Peace" was published in *Musings* in the Fall of 1990.

"An Insinuation" was written February 10 – 17, 1955. The reference in it is to Mark Antony in Shakespeare's "Julius Caesar".

"Campus-5:15 p.m." was written as a reaction to an atheist who was an official chaplain at Penn State University, and bears the note at the bottom of the page "How does the Devil manage to do this?"

"Childsong" was published in *Musings* on September 17, 2000.

"Choice" was written as the ninth poem of ten assignments in the spring semester of 1955.

"Creation" was published in Musings October 18, 1987.

"Dancers" was written for children.

"Earth-Cry" is from December, 1954.

"Earth-Cry (II)" is from February 17 – 24, 1955. This poem is a reworking of the first version (above) to meet the requirements of a Penn State Poetry

Composition class that taught: "Today we don't write such form-following poetry" as Sonnets, which I think it was.

"Easter House" was written March 24, 2001.

"Hush" was written for children.

"Idyll" was the seventh poem of ten assignments from spring of 1955.

"Inquiry" was written January, 1955.

"Kairos": kairos – A time when conditions are right for the accomplishment of a crucial action; the opportune and decisive moment – *Webster's 3rd New International Dictionary Unabridged* (1966).

"Lifestream" was published in *Musings* April 1, 1990.

"May all your swains" was written for Taylor Gerhard's birthday card January 30, 2002.

"Mystery" was written January, 1954.

"Night Walk" was published in *Musings* November 12, 1995.

"Oh Dear" was published in *Musings* March 25, 1990.

"Perception" is from March, 1954.

"Sheeta": The title for the poem was borrowed from Tarzan's "ape language" or from the Kipling books.

"Sleeping Off the Cold Morning" are lyrics for a song given to Fred and Rachael Gerhard.

"Spring Breaks" was written for Easter cards March 25, 2002.

"Thanksgiving" was written late fall, 2003.

"The Perfect Place" was submitted to *The Reading Eagle* September 10, 1999.

"The Waves" was completed April 2005.

"This Snow" was written mid-January 2003.

"To My Favorite Mother" is from October, 1953.

"Traces" was written April 14, 2005.

"Two Candles Burning" are lyrics written for Fred and Rachael Gerhard's wedding, and was sung by Fred and Rachael at their wedding reception.

"Virtual Mate" was written March 21, 1998.

"When the Good Lord tried to tell us" was written for Calvin Gerhard for a Father's Day card.

"Wild One": remuda - horses from which are chosen those to be used for the day by the ranch hands – *Webster's 3rd New International Dictionary Unabridged* (1966).

"You Don't Know Me, But--" was written in the summer of 1953.

ACKNOWLEDGEMENTS

Many of these poems were originally published in *Musings*, the poetry column of *The Reading Eagle*, including "Absurd," "Accepting Peace," "Childsong," "Creation," "Lifestream," "Night Walk," and "Oh Dear." And "Dancers" was featured on *Bespoke Vocals* on YouTube, read by the actor Kirk Lawrence-Howard. Deep gratitude to Calvin Gerhard for permission to publish Rena's work and for the cover photograph.

ABOUT THE AUTHOR

Rena Gerhard's poems were published frequently in *Musings (The Reading Eagle)*. She also had her poetry featured in an episode of *Bespoke Vocals* on YouTube. She started writing at an early age, and for nearly 60 years. She received her bachelors degree in English from Penn State University where she went on to earn a masters degree in Philosophy. She did coursework towards a doctorate in English at Penn State, and taught Logic at the Penn State Campus in Altoona, PA. A composer of hymns and counterpoint pieces, she also enjoyed folk dancing, ballroom dancing, and in her youth, ballet. She lived in Pennsylvania with her husband and sons primarily as a homemaker, dance instructor, and Sunday school teacher. Rena frequently expressed her joy in family life, and in a love of Jesus and God. She was an inspiration to those around her to follow their creative endeavors fully, to make music, sing, dance — and yes — to write poetry.